Pick the Very BEST
SHELLEY A.W. ROY

Published by Five Crows Publishing

Book Design by and

Illustrated by Shelley A.W. Roy

ISBN: 978-0-9844314-5-8

This book is dedicated to my two grandsons – Edison & Theo. May they always feel loved and know that they can create the life of their dreams.

A special thank you to Mrs. Romero's 2nd grade class

at Gulliver Prep for sharing their thoughts.

Tell your secret.

It's exciting!

Thinking is hard.

Don't listen.

A free trip to Hawaii!

You have to go to bed.

I'm invited to a party!

Have you ever thought about thoughts?

Why do some thoughts drift slowly on by
and others flit past like a butterfly

while others stop as if to say,

"Hi!"

Or have you wondered
how they can swirl,
and twirl,
and spin
around
inside?
@MiamiEdGuru

Some seem light

And why do a handful
shout?
PICK ME!
PICK ME!
@MiamiEdGuru

Then there are times
thoughts whisper softly.

Tempting your mind which can be costly.

Or times when too many crowd-in
pushing and shoving trying
to capture your attention

creating a lot of tension.

Once in a while they wiggle
and jiggle and tickle inside you.

Begging you to tittle, and giggle
and spittle outside you.

Have you ever been lucky and grabbed
a thought that sparkled so bright
that you felt brilliant and oh, so right?

Not often enough one comes around that is so profound you just have to SIT DOWN!

Have you ever noticed that when a thought STICKS the harder you push it away the stronger it gets!

SO WHAT CAN YOU DO
WHEN A THOUGHT GETS STUCK?

Picture it in a bubble
floating away
higher and higher
POOF
there it goes.
@MiamiEdGuru

Grab some paper-
write it down-
draw it out
put it in a box.
DON'T LET IT OUT!

Place a Belly Buddy on your tummy.
Breathe deep –
up-down-up-down.

Soon your breath will slow down.
Then the thought's no longer around.

GO CRAZY!

Use your imagination.

GO CRAZY!

Give it a stinky smell.

GO CRAZY!

Then laugh, and laugh, and laugh
as it rolls down an imaginary hill.

You might just find
that one of the best
things about thoughts

is the space in between.

Where you breathe deep

and create peaceful dreams.

But you know what
the very best
thing about thoughts is?

You get to
decide which
to HANG ONTO.

@MiamiEdGuru

Which to
LET GO OF,
@MiamiEdguru

Which to HUG
and keep close
by your side.
@MiamiEdGuru

So my advice
PICK THE VERY BEST!

Dear Reader,

Remember you are the creator of your life: one thought, one action, one day at a time. May your life be filled with rainbows and flowers.

Remember don't ever dream about fuzzy pink bunnies.

Shelley

About the Author

Shelley Roy was destined to be a teacher from the age of four, when she had a classroom in her basement. She has spent over 44 years in the profession, and as a student once wrote on her door –

After working in the Mecklenburg County Jail, Shelley became even more dedicated to helping young people realize they can take control of their own lives.

Although Ms. Roy has lived in nine different states and two countries, she considers Minnesota her heart home.

She has two sons, a daughter in-law and two grandsons. The Fourth of July at the family cabin on Twin Lakes is her favorite.

Humans only use 10% of their brain.
Wait — I know that answer.
Ooh yeah a stuffed animal.
INTERRUPT!
My brain hurts.
Chicken wings — chicken wings
Why am I here?

www.ingramcontent.com/pod-product-compliance
Lightning Source LLC
Chambersburg PA
CBHW042054030726
47599CB00019B/2484